This book belongs to:

The Letterlanders

Annie Apple	Bouncy Ben	Clever Cat	Dippy Duck	Eddy Elephant	Fireman Fred	Golden Girl

Hairy Hat Man	Impy Ink	Jumping Jim	Kicking King	Lucy Lamp Lady	Munching Mike

Naughty Nick	Oscar Orange	Poor Peter	Quarrelsome Queen	Robber Red	Sammy Snake	Ticking Tess

Uppy Umbrella	Vase of Violets	Wicked Water Witch	Max and Maxine	Yellow Yo-yo Man	Zig Zag Zebra

Letterland™

First Alphabet and Word Book

TED SMART

This edition produced for The Book People Ltd,
Hall Wood Avenue, Haydock, St Helens, WA11 9UL

Published by Collins Educational
An imprint of HarperCollins*Publishers* Ltd
77-85 Fulham Palace Road
London W6 8JB

© Lyn Wendon 1998

First published in this format 1998
Alphabet Adventures first published 1996
First Picture Word Book first published 1997

ISBN 0 583 33803 8

LETTERLAND® is a registered trademark of Lyn Wendon.

Jane Launchbury asserts the moral right to be identified as the author of *Alphabet Adventures*.
Lyn Wendon asserts the moral right to be identified as the author of *First Picture Word Book*.

Alphabet Adventures
Designer: Michael Sturley
Illustrator: Jane Launchbury
Colourist: Dulce Tobin
Consultant: Lyn Wendon, originator of Letterland

First Picture Word Book
Designer: Sally Boothroyd
Illustrator: Anna Jupp
Colourist: Gina Hart
Consultant: Lyn Wendon, originator of Letterland

British Library Cataloguing in Publication Data
A catalogue record for this book is available from the British Library.

Printed by Scotprint Ltd, Musselburgh, Scotland.

Alphabet Adventures

Written and illustrated
by Jane Launchbury

At the seaside

'A day by the sea is good for me,'
Says Sammy Snake sleepily.
All his Letterland friends agree.
How many of them can you see?

Off to the fair!

Let's all go to the Letterland fair!
But how shall we get from here to there?
Ticking Tess will take the train,
Poor Peter prefers to go by plane.
Robber Red races on roller skates.
Can you find his Letterland mates?

Let's go shopping!

Sammy Snake is selling sweets,
Ticking Tess is buying treats.
Oscar Orange has lost his brother,
Munching Mike stays close to his mother.
While you search for all the rest,
Which of the shops do you like best?

13

Jungle adventure

High up in the jungle trees
Jumping Jim says 'Help me, please.
Help me find my Letterland chums
Before the hungry tiger comes!'

At the airport

Jumping Jim is shouting 'Hooray!'
He's just off on a holiday.
Some of his friends are coming back.
But what is that in Robber Red's sack?

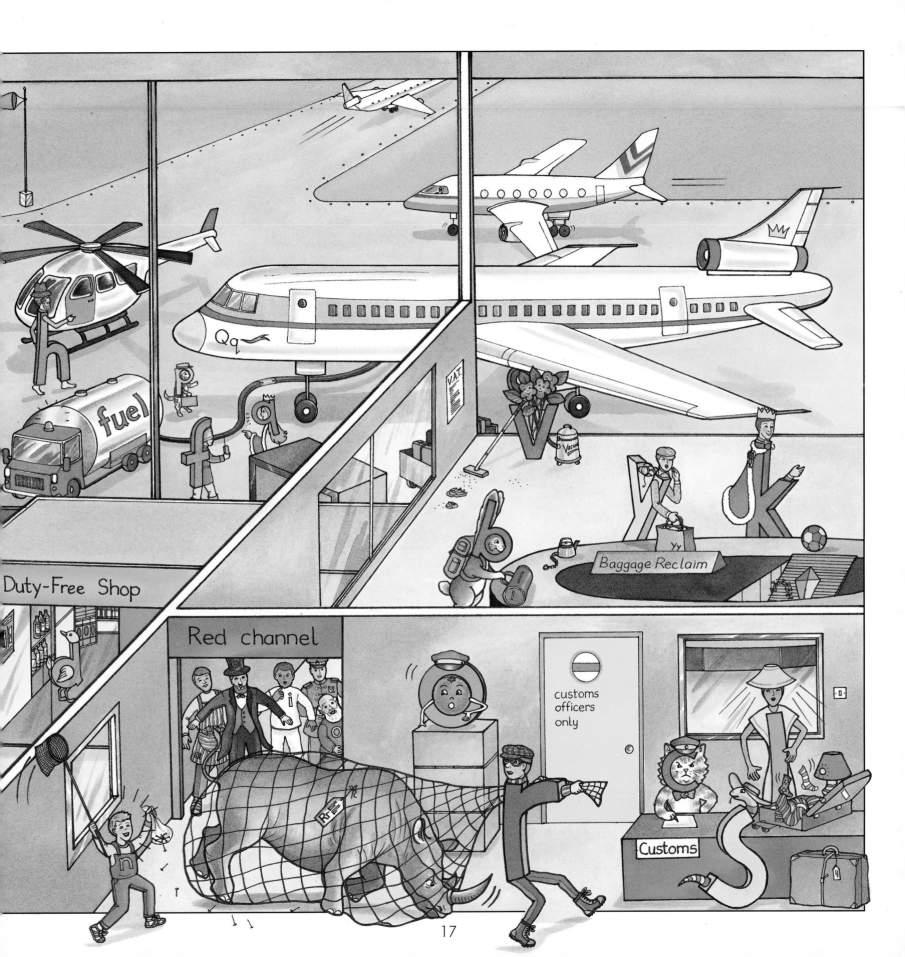

Duty-Free Shop

Red channel

Baggage Reclaim

V.A.T.

customs
officers
only

Customs

fuel

17

Down by the river

Lamp Lady Lucy is on her way
To join us on this sunny day.
What do you think she'd like to eat
As a special picnic treat?

Fun on the farm

Down on the farm there's Bouncy Ben.
He's busy feeding a noisy hen.
Behind the barn, poor Ticking Tess
Is cleaning up a nasty mess!
Most of their friends are busy too.
The bird can see them all, can you?

Classroom chaos

Who can it be in the Letterland school
That's broken one important rule?
Never let a rhino loose
Without a very good excuse!

23

In hospital

Oh dear, dear! Poor Fireman Fred!
He fell downstairs and bumped his head.
Sammy Snake ate too much cake
And now he's got a tummy ache!
Look at the picture. Can you say
What's going on in the hospital today?

Accident & Emergency

Healthy
Hearts

Operating Theatre

LETTERLAND
HOSPITAL

ward 1
ward 2
ward 3
ward 4

A & E
X-Ray
Pharmacy
Shop
Toilets

X-Ray

Patients' Pills

Ward 3

25

Playing in the park

Poor Peter Puppy is happy today.
He's in the park and he's ready to play.
Most of his friends are having fun,
But can you spot the unlucky one?

At the zoo

Can you hear the hullabaloo
Coming from the Letterland Zoo?
Join us there to see what's new...
A lovely baby kangaroo!

Hot House

28

It's party time!

Quarrelsome Queen would like to invite
You all to her fancy dress party tonight.
Now she is wondering who is who.
Search for every little clue!

Quarrelsome Queen's questions

Can you find a picture of...

1   Annie Apple covered in ants?

2   Bouncy Ben being a butterfly?

3   Clever Cat looking cross?

4   Dippy Duck in a drawer?

5   Eddy Elephant and eleven eggs?

6   Fireman Fred holding a flag?

7   Golden Girl holding a bunch of green grapes?

8   Hairy Hat Man without his hat on?

9   Impy Ink and six big insects?

10 Jumping Jim doing a jigsaw?

11 Kicking King with a bunch of keys?

12 Lucy Lamp Lady looking for a lost lamb?

13 Munching Mike in a motorboat?

14 Naughty Nick being a nice nurse?

15 Oscar Orange with an orang-utan?

16 Poor Peter eating a piece of pork pie?

17 Quarrelsome Queen quarrelling with a squirrel?

18 Robber Red rowing on a river?

19 Sammy Snake and a scarecrow?

20 Ticking Tess talking to a tiger?

21 Uppy Umbrella looking unhappy?

22 Vase of Violets on a video camera?

23 Wicked Water Witch wading in the water?

24 Max and Maxine in a taxi?

25 Yellow Yo-yo Man yawning?

26 Zig Zag Zebra zipping up a bag?

The Letterland alphabet is the basis of the well-known Letterland system for the teaching of reading used in the majority of English primary schools.

Letterland™

First
Picture
Word Book

A a

astronaut

address

Annie Apple,
Apple Tree House,
Apple Town,
Letterland.

alligator

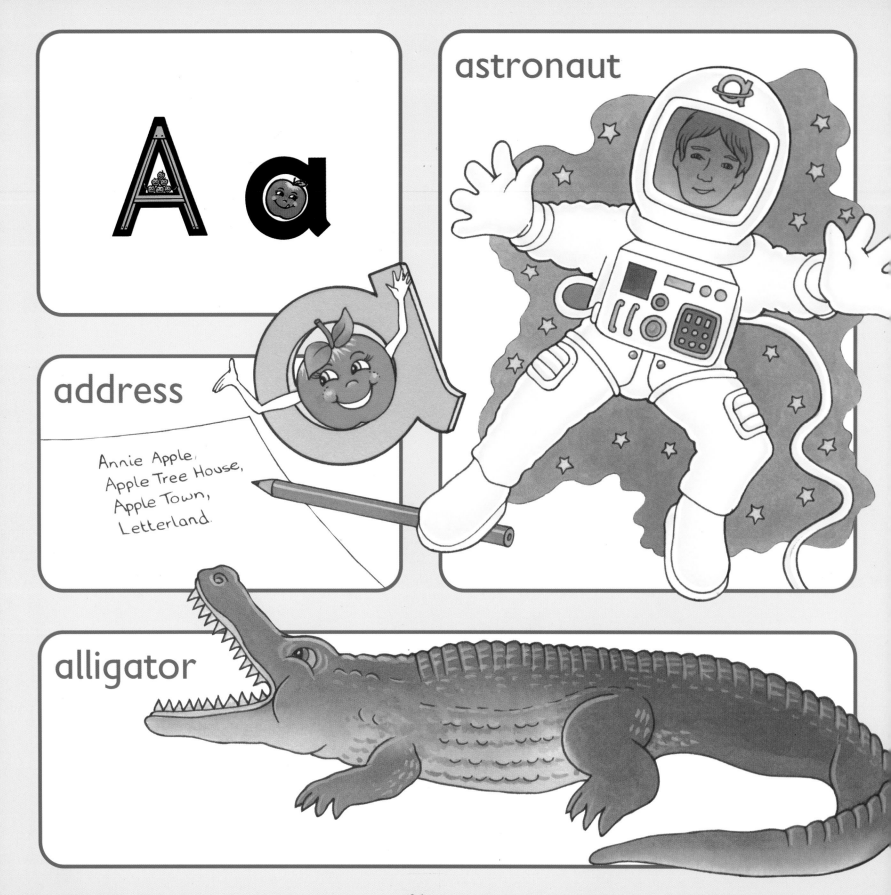

acrobats

ambulance

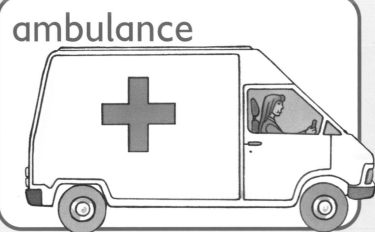

ants

apple

alphabet

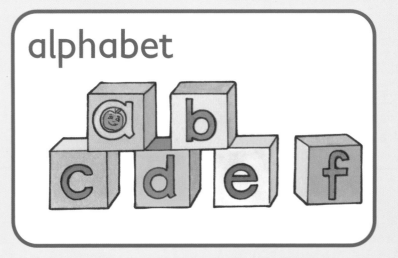

37

B b

baby

bus

banana

butterfly

book

38

birthday

B b

birds

buttons

bell

bike

39

coat

clown

cake

crayons

cow

C c

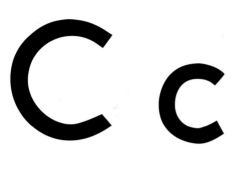

clock

cup

Christmas

D d

doctor

dressing up

doll

dice

drum

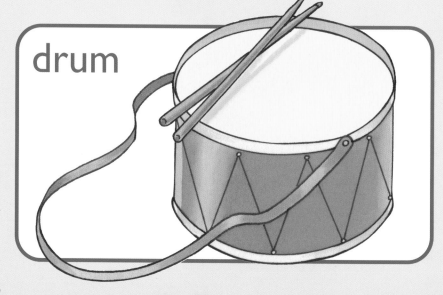

dinosaur

D d

donkey

digger

dog

E e

eggs

elephant

envelope

escalator

EXIT

44

E e

flower

football

fireworks

farm

fish

F f

45

glasses

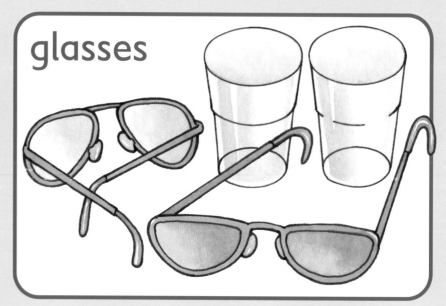

guitar

gloves

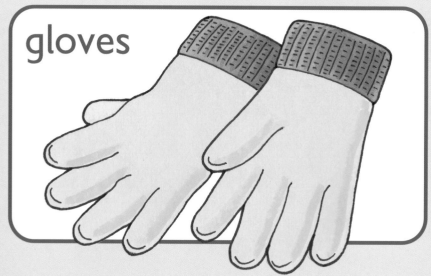

goose

gate

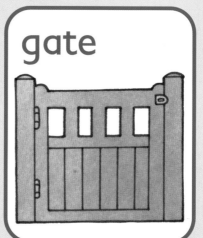

green

grapes

G g

garden

goldfish

guinea pig

47

H h

helicopter

horse

hat

hedgehog

48

hens

H h

handstand

hammer

house

49

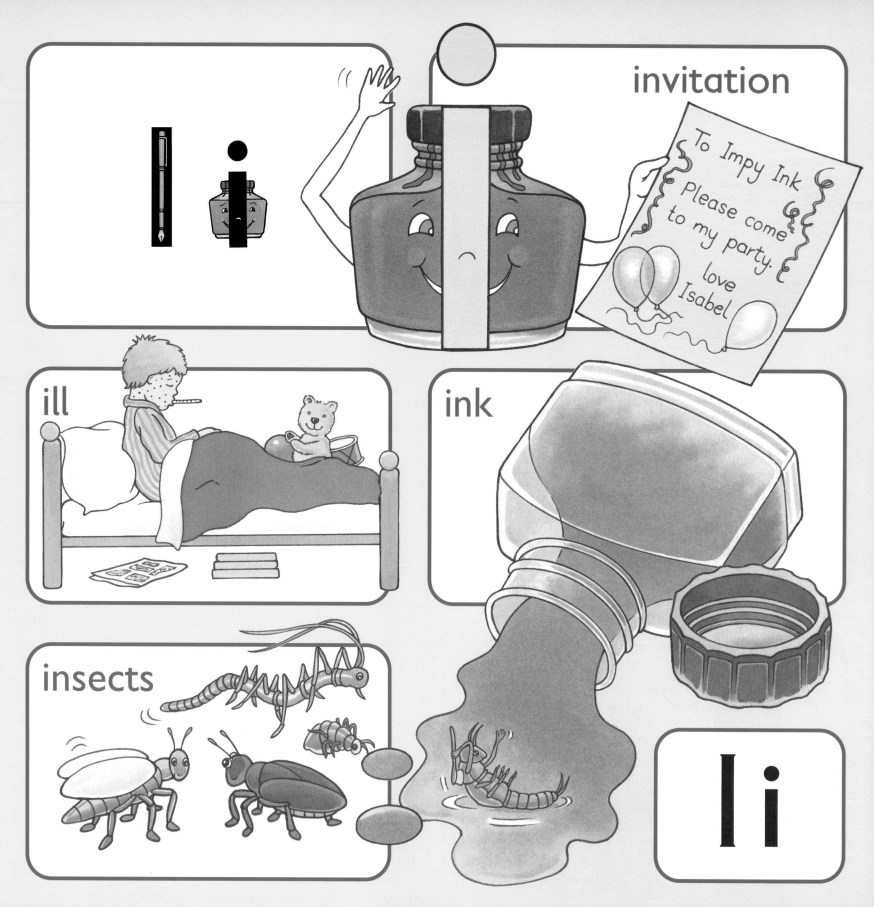

invitation

ill

ink

insects

Ii

jet

jug

jelly

jam

jigsaw

jeans

J j

51

K k

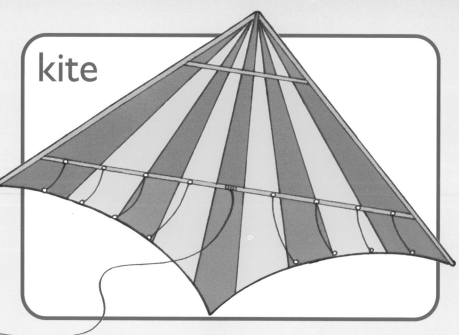

kite

king

kettle

key

kittens

koala

K k

kiss

kangaroo

kitchen

lorry

lambs

lighthouse

ladder

leaf

Ll

lollipop

letter

Dear Lucy,
It was lovely to
see you last week
at the library.
Let's get together
for lunch soon.

love,
Linda.

Lucy Lamp
Letterla...
Lighthou...

lion

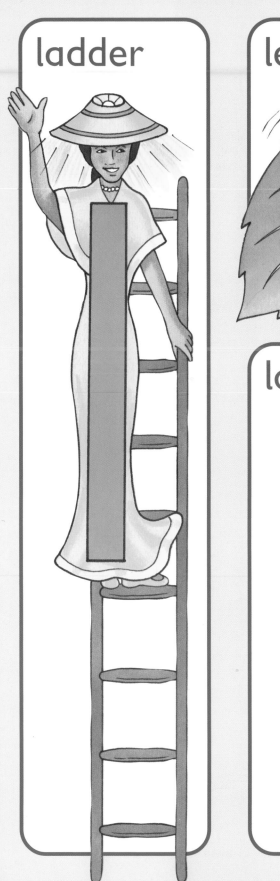

M m

mountain

monkey

marbles

magnet

56

mouse

mole

M m

milk

mushroom

MILK

mirror

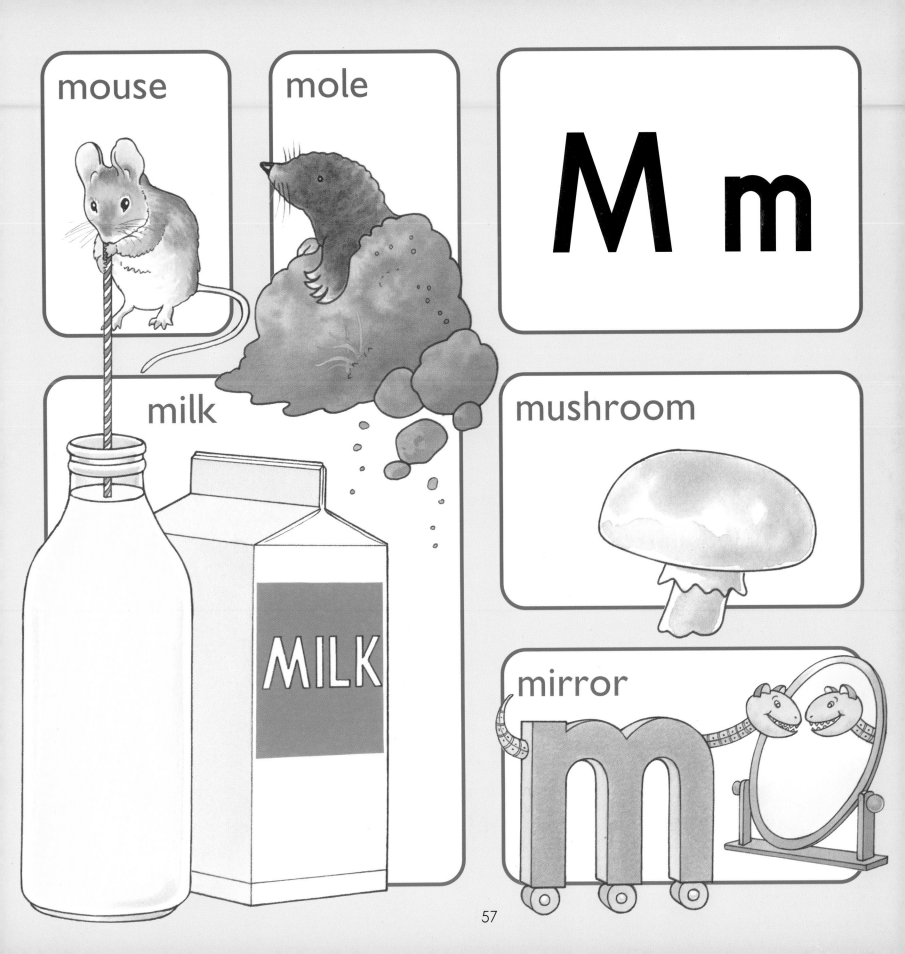

N n

night

needle

net

nuts

nest

nine

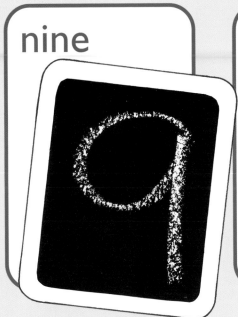

nails

N n

necklace

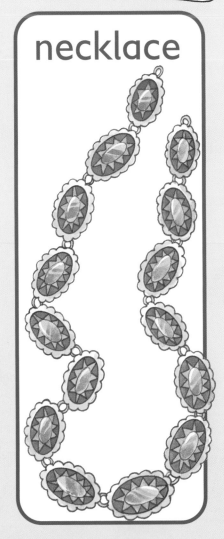

noodles

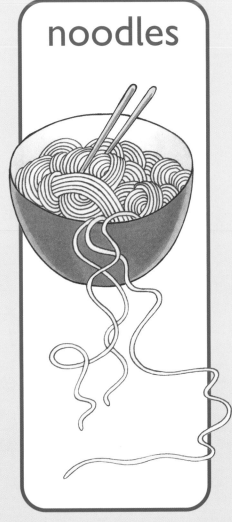

nurse

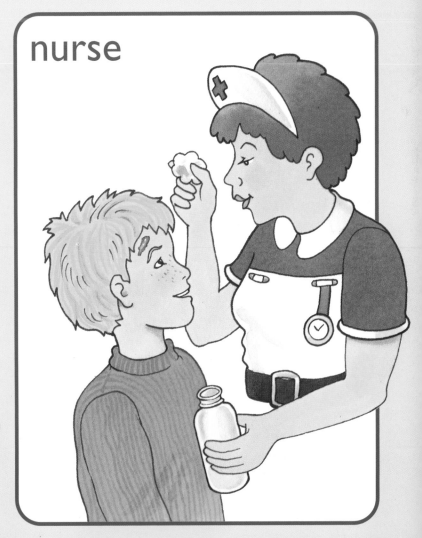

octopus

October

oblong box

60

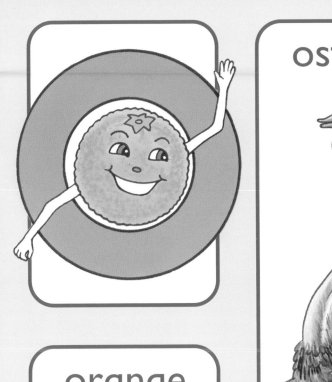

ostrich

O o

orange

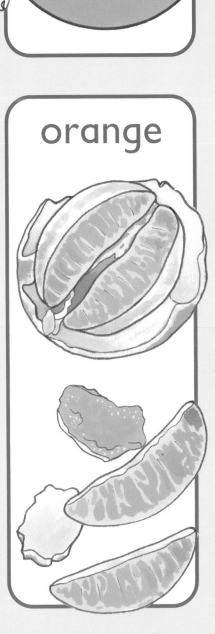

otter

P p

picture

parrot

playground

pattern

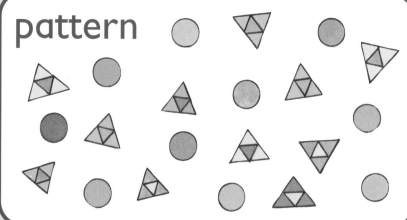

panda

P p

pear

plum

puppies

peach

peas

present

63

quads

queen

quilt

quarter

Qq

rainbow

robot

rose

rollerblades

rabbit

Rr

S s

sausages

snowman

socks

snail

spider

spaceship

S s

strawberry

seaside

toothbrush

toothpaste

television

trees

teddy

tiger

tomato

teapot

T t

toys

torch

tractor

69

U u

umbrella

upside down

underwear

underwater

U u

Vv

violin

volcano

van

vegetables

video

V v

71

worms

web

windmill

watch

wall

W w

X x

taxi

exercise

six

6

fox

boxes

X x

73

yellow

yawn

yacht

yoghurt

yo-yos

Y y

zip

zig-zag

zoo

zebra crossing

Z z

HERE ARE SOME MORE LETTERLAND TITLES ...

... FOR YOU TO ENJOY

The Letterland alphabet is the basis of the well-known Letterland system for the teaching of reading used in the majority of English primary schools.

Letterland™

Letterland At Home is a range of books, cassettes and flashcards that uses a fun approach to help children to read and write. Three colour-coded Stages will help you to choose the books that are right for your child.

Stage 1

Stage 2

Available from all good bookshops.

For an information leaflet about Letterland call 0181 307 4052.

Stage 3

For younger children, a colourful range of first skills activity books has been developed.